ST PETER PO
a brief histo₁

by

Gregory Stevens Cox

FORESAY

St Peter Port is remarkable. It can boast two royal castles, a fine medieval church, Calvinistic links with Geneva, Civil War drama. Its privateers rivalled those of St Malo and it became a major international entrepôt in the Georgian era. Mercantile wealth funded architectural improvement and St Peter Port boasts handsome Regency buildings. Discerning visitors of the Romantic era enjoyed the picturesque quality of St Peter Port's setting with its fine maritime vistas. The town was home to Victor Hugo for over fifteen years and inspired paragraphs in *The Toilers of the Sea*. Today St Peter Port welcomes thousands of visitors. Some – admiring its beautiful setting, Georgian architecture, and rich history – have suggested that the town deserves to be designated a world heritage site.

To attempt in a few pages to tell the story of eight centuries of a town's existence is a rash enterprise. This monograph is inevitably a sketch. I have tried to explain the evolution of St Peter Port, concentrating on the underlying logic that fashioned the town's character. For those who wish to delve more deeply I have drawn attention to significant books and essays in the *Bibliography and Notes* section.

This sketch would not have been possible without the research of many dedicated local archaeologists and historians, past and present – I pay tribute to them. I thank Tim Furmidge for his help in creating the map of medieval St Peter Port and Mikal Dyas for his depiction of furniture (p. 33). I thank all those who have kindly helped my research – Richard Hocart, David Le Conte, Roy Bisson, Richard Platt, Graham Jackson; Amanda Bennett and the staff of the Priaulx Library; Dr Darryl Ogier and the staff of the Island Archive Service; Dr Jason Monaghan and the staff of the Island Museum and Heritage Service. I thank all those who have attended my lectures over the years, their questions have stimulated my research.

The author is presently composing a fuller history of St Peter Port. Those wishing to subscribe may write to –

toucan.guernsey@gmail.com

Subscribers will receive a discount when the book is published. No money will be payable until published.

Hoc opusculum Rosemariae gratissime dedico.

CONTENTS

1. Beginnings

People have been living in the St Peter Port area since the prehistoric period. Why did they choose this location? There are three important reasons.

First, there were streams flowing down from the west. This was a convenient source of drinking water. Then, in the medieval era, the water-power of the streams was harnessed to drive several mills – the high technology of the period. Finally, in the early modern period, the streams were useful to the woolworkers of the town.

Secondly, the summit of the hill to the west overlooked the sea. The approach of a hostile fleet could be sighted in good time and the hill afforded a convenient strong-point for defence.

Thirdly, the bay provided a natural anchorage. Herm and Jethou provided shelter from blustery easterlies.

By the first century BC cargo vessels trading between the continent and Hengistbury Head in Dorset were sailing *via* Guernsey. There is good archaeological evidence of occupation and trade during the Roman period. Such evidence has been found at the Plaiderie, in the harbour, and in the market area.

There is little evidence, archaeological or historical, about the island during the 'Dark Ages'. The story becomes easier to trace by the eleventh century. Norman documents of that era refer to the church of St Peter Port. Peter was one of Christ's first disciples, a fisherman. As such, he was an obvious patron saint for a church hard by the sea. In the eleventh and twelfth centuries St Peter Port was little more than a fishing village. The island market was situated not in St Peter Port but in the Castel parish – a central location easy of access to all islanders.

2. From fishing village to town with royal castles

Properly to understand the story of St Peter Port it is essential to recognise the geo-political situation in the thirteenth century. In 1204 King John lost his duchy of Normandy to Philippe Auguste, the French king. The Channel Islands were the only parts of the duchy that John managed to retain. The islands now required special attention, they were vulnerable to French raids. If John and his successor Henry III were to keep the remnants of their Norman duchy, they had to make proper military provision. Initially the English crown established a strong-point at Ivy Castle in the parish of St Peter Port. The castle was surrounded by marshes and could easily be defended against assaults. However it was not perfect.

The English crown had lost mainland Normandy but still held extensive territories in south-west France. The English king ruled a maritime empire stretching from the Scottish borders to Gascony. Guernsey became a vital post in the communication network. Ships travelling on royal business north and south could touch at Guernsey for shelter, supplies, instructions. Ivy Castle was poorly located to fulfil such a maritime role and it was superseded. By the 1240s it was referred to as the old castle, Castle Cornet was the new castle. This new castle was excellently situated. It had a commanding view of the approaches to St Peter Port and was easy of access to seafarers. Officials at the castle could monitor vessels trading in and out of St Peter Port. Set on an island, the castle provided secure protection for cash and documents.

It was at this stage that St Peter Port metamorphosed from village to town. St Peter Port with its strategic position in the Anglo-Gallic world became a significant port. Castle Cornet also promoted urban development. It had more than a military function, it was a residence for officials and acted as an estate office. The castle population of officials, soldiers, and servants required supplies and services – and that stimulated the local economy.

The town also served the king's purpose by housing his *grange*. To this the islanders delivered agricultural produce – feudal dues owed to *fief le roi*. The king held four water-mills and one windmill in the parish. Mills were vital in the medieval economy. They generated power, principally for the grinding of cereals. The owner of a mill controlled a valuable asset and could make a good income by charging for the use of the facility.

In the second half of the 13th century St Peter Port was no longer like the other Guernsey parishes with their farmers and fishermen. St Peter Port housed soldiers and officials, craftsmen, traders and specialists. In the past historians used to define a town by reference to the nature of land tenure and privileges held. These legal concepts distinguished the urban community from the large village. St Peter Port did not enjoy privileges, nor a charter conferring urban status, it lacked the municipal institutions characteristic of the fully developed medieval town. However, it can be defined as a town if we use criteria adduced by urban historians today – diversity of occupation and regular markets.

St Peter Port had started as a fishing centre. A fish market was held on Tuesdays, Thursdays, and Saturdays but the general market of the island was situated the Castel parish. As St Peter Port grew in importance in the thirteenth century, there was increasing pressure for it to hold the general market. This was eventually effected in 1309. The market was approximately one acre in size, it was defined as

> an area containing 2.5 virgates [= *about one acre*] of land for a long time lying as uncultivated pasture, the north end abutting the spring called La Fontaine Cache Vassal, the other end abutting Le Vaal Wydecok', the king's highway cuts across it almost in the middle (Le Patourel 1935, p. 196, translated).

It lay just to the west of the High Street.

Apart from the market there were also shops in St Peter Port. Records for 1331 refer to 41 wine-sellers, 12 beer-sellers, and 70 bakers being punished for breaking the assizes of wine, beer and bread. The figures seem surprisingly high – we should perhaps remember that these sellers were supplying not just the urban population but also the crews of visiting vessels. Moreover ship captains undoubtedly bought rations in St Peter Port sufficient for voyages lasting days or weeks.

The harbour was busy. In the eleven months ending on 29 August 1330 custom was levied on 487 foreign ships putting in at St Peter Port. Many of these vessels were freighting wine from Bordeaux to England. St Peter Port was a convenient 'half-way' point for breaking the voyage and obtaining fresh victuals. Sometimes wine was unloaded at Guernsey and reshipped to ports in Normandy and Brittany – St Peter Port was serving as an entrepôt. Besides wine, the Guernsey merchants exported fish and cereals. The economic activity around the harbour was sufficiently intense to bring into being at least two kinds of specialists – *portitores* and *bermanni* – men who worked as porters and handled wine casks.

St Peter Port was a frontier town vulnerable to raids by the French. One such attack in 1294 brought considerable destruction. St Peter Port suffered on the outbreak of the Hundred Years War. The castle was seized by the French early in the war and was held for several years. In the mid-14th century the king ordered that the town should be walled. This measure was for the protection of the town and its inhabitants. The king derived an income from the port and had every incentive to defend his interests. To what extent the wall was constructed is not clear. The walls of houses may have been built to serve as sections of the town wall. A tower was constructed at Beauregard. This housed a garrison that was on hand to defend the town.

The town was small in its physical extent. It is still relatively easy to determine the boundaries of the medieval community. The barrières stones approximately mark the perimeter of the old town. Examples of these are to be found near the Town Church, in Smith Street, and in the Pollet. The laws of inheritance in St Peter Port were different from those that prevailed throughout the rest of the island. Consequently it was vital for advocates to know whether a property lay inside or outside the town boundaries – within or without the barrières stones.

Apart from the Town Church there were a number of chapels in the parish. A French document refers to the chapel of the blessed Michael in the manor of St Peter Port. By the Tourgand there was a chapel and hostelry for pilgrims, founded in 1361 and dedicated to St

Julian, patron saint of travellers. Close to where Elizabeth College now stands – and outside the town boundaries – there was a Franciscan friary with its church. Also in the parish (and outside the town) were a *chapelle de Lorette* and a chapel dedicated to St Jacques. Castle Cornet housed a chapel, as did Ivy Castle.

The population of St Peter Port probably fluctuated from a high point in the first half of the 14th century to a lower figure after the devastation of the Black Death (1348). The Black Death not only killed many, it left in its wake living victims. This is perhaps what inspired Peter of St Peter Port in 1350 to found a hospital 'at Bowez in the parish of St. Pierre Port' and to endow it.

Port towns regularly contained a diverse population and St Peter Port was no exception. Town dwellers speaking their Norman patois mixed with fellow islanders visiting the market, Gascon merchants, English soldiers on garrison duty, Norman and Breton seafarers, preaching friars from France, and itinerant pilgrims.

3. A Godly town, visited by plagues and punishments

From the late 15th century until the late 17th century Guernsey enjoyed neutrality. This was thanks to a Vatican edict that forbade fighting in Channel Islands waters. St Peter Port consequently enjoyed a favourable status as a trading port during wartime. Both the English and their enemies could use the town for buying and selling produce. Nevertheless, there was a continual anxiety that St Peter Port was vulnerable to attack. For that reason Castle Cornet was well maintained. In the Tudor era major improvements were made to the castle fortifications. New architectural features were introduced, principally to defend the castle from the challenge of guns and artillery – the new military technology.

The population of St Peter Port was in the region of 1,000 – 2,000 for much of this period. There were, however, considerable fluctuations. At intervals there were outbreaks of plague and rates of death reached 'crisis mortality' level. In October 1546 an *ordonnance* was issued forbidding plague victims attending places of public assembly such as churches. There was a high level of mortality in 1580 and 1583. In 1590-1591 there were so many deaths in St Peter Port that the authorities found it impossible to register the burials properly.

There was constant vigilance surrounding foreigners entering town and the island. A foreigner might be a French spy. Or he might be poor and become a liability to the community. An *ordonnance* of 1537 directed the Prevost du Roy to superintend the arrival of vessels from Jersey, Normandy, and other parts; to keep a record of the names of passengers disembarking; and to keep an eye on them until they left. The *ordonnance* also required that strangers living in Guernsey for more than a year who could not subsist without begging were to leave or risk being whipped.

During the reign of Queen Mary three women were sentenced to death for continuing in heresy. Guillemine Gilbert and Perotine Massey and their mother Catherine Cauchés were executed in July 1556. As they were being consumed by the flames of the fire, Perotine gave premature birth. The bailiff plucked up the new born baby and cast it into the flames, on the pretext that it was a heretic.

This episode harmed Catholicism in Guernsey and the town turned to Protestantism. The parish was administered following a Presbyterian system modelled on Calvinism. This afforded an escape from the episcopal bureaucracy of Catholic Coutances and then Anglican Winchester. The authorities suppressed Catholicism. Pilgrims were fined. An *ordonnance* of 1571 banned *choses superstitieuses* on the 1st of November – All Saints' Day, a holyday of obligation for Catholics. Calvinistic morality was imposed in much the same way as in Scotland and on the Continent. There were injunctions against singing and dancing. The authorities were keen that rank should be properly observed and they introduced sumptuary legislation. An *ordonnance* forbade servants wearing velvet, silk, silver, and various ornaments. There was a campaign against sexual immorality. Pre-marital sex was discouraged. Fiancés were forbidden to live with their fiancées before the marriage was solemnised. Adultery was punished severely as it threatened the sanctity of marriage. A punishment of three weeks in prison was prescribed for adulterous men. Each Saturday of that prison term the culprit would be exposed in the cage in town from 9 a.m. until sunset. The cage was a wooden structure, somewhat like an enormous parrot-cage. Those inside were exposed to humiliation and verbal abuse from the crowd. Having emerged from the cage, the culprit was whipped at the 'quarrefours de la ville', receiving 24 lashes. On the final Saturday the whipping was to draw blood. Females were sentenced to 24 lashes at the beginning of their sentence, and to three Saturdays in the cage.

Elizabeth College was founded in 1563. The school hours were from 7am to 11am and from 1pm to 5pm in the summer, from 8am in the winter. There were six forms. The curriculum centred on the teaching of Latin; Greek was started in the third form. An interesting feature of the curriculum in the 4th form was the study of a Greek author alongside a similar Latin author – Hesiod alongside Vergil, Pindar parallel with Horace. The 5th form studied oratory – Isocrates and Cicero – and the 6th form read historians – Thucydides, Herodotus, Sallust, and Livy. The statutes saw translation from French into Latin as an important technique for mastering the classical language. (French, not English, was the vernacular language of the town.) The Principal of the College was required to be a man of good character and could be removed if guilty of 'theft, homicide, perjury, heresy, fornication, adultery, drunkenness, or gluttony.'

One of the first Principals of the college was Adrian Saravia, an academic with a European reputation. His days in Guernsey were not happy. He complained bitterly, recording that while preaching in the country he was pelted with dung. His protestantism was presumably unwelcome to traditionalists clinging to the old faith. Saravia's prayers were answered – he was invited to join the team in England that produced the great King James translation of the Bible (1611).

4. Stuart strife

St Peter Port experienced mixed fortunes in the seventeenth century. Plague continued to trouble the town and there were mortality crises in 1606, 1615, 1626 and 1629-1630.

An act of the Royal Court of 26 August 1629 ordered that those suffering from the plague should be lodged at the Maladrie by the lands of Jean de Quetteville, at Rocques-ès-Chevres and that corpses of plague victims should be interred at the Cimetière des Frères (at the time employed as a garden by Thomas Blanche). By segregating the living victims and by using plague pits for the dead, the Guernsey authorities were following strategies well tested in many European cities.

Town life was carefully regulated. Tudor strictures about begging, drunkenness, and fornication were repeated. There were measures to deter foreigners settling on the island, residence required the permission of the Governor. The authorities oversaw the weights, measures, and quality of provisions offered by butchers, bakers, fishmongers, and tavern-keepers. Householders in town were required on Wednesdays and Saturdays to clean the street or lane abutting their property. Gambling was frowned upon, and an *ordonnance* of 1613-4 made provision for the restitution of losses greater than 60 sous.

There were urban improvements. In 1625 Jean de Quetteville was instructed to bring 'un paveur' to pave the streets. An *ordonnance* of 1628 ruled that new building schemes required permission from the Constable and six members of the douzaine.

The authorities eagerly promoted Protestantism. There was a hunt to find and destroy any Papist books that remained in private possession. Sundays were to be kept holy; taverns, dancing, and racy songs were forbidden (*Ordonnances*, 1614-15, 1635, 1653).

There was friction between the islanders and the English government. Defying English diktat, the islanders grew their own tobacco, thereby depriving the English of tax revenues on imported tobacco. The islanders for their part were disgruntled that the English failed to check Moorish pirates who harassed shipping in the Channel.

When the English Civil War broke out in 1642 the islanders had divided loyalties. Some prominent families declared for Parliament but Royalists held Castle Cornet. There was consequently a local civil war, castle *versus* town. Some attempts were made to storm the castle but they failed. For their part the castle soldiers fired a great many cannonballs at St Peter Port. The townsfolk took defensive measures – States meetings were moved westwards from the Plaiderie, out of gun-range. The bombardments created some physical damage but apparently only two people were killed – one of whom supported the king! Eventually Parliament emerged triumphant in England. Subsequently the Channel Islands were swiftly brought to heel.

5. Better days

On the Restoration in 1660, Charles II graciously pardoned Guernsey for having sided with the enemies of his father. From this time onwards the economic fortunes of Guernsey steadily improved. The merchants of St Peter Port became involved in the international trade that centred on St Malo. The Malouins were making fortunes in Cadiz, trading northern produce for silver imported from South America. There was also an extensive trade between St Malo and England. Textiles, lace, oil, soap, hemp, cordage, and honey were exported from St Malo to England; in return the Malouins imported draperies, tin, lead, coal, slate, hides, beef, herring, sardines, and tallow. The Malouins distrusted the English and used Guernsey merchants to handle much of their cross-Channel freight.

Late in September 1677 Charles Trumbull arrived with friends in St Peter Port. Being asked whence they came

> and it being answered from Jersey, the whole company at the Pier… rudely saluted us with that mock word 'de Jersey' by way of contempt and scorn, which shows that there is no great kindness between the two neighbouring rival islands. (Hocart 1985 for all the Trumbull references).

Inter-insular badinage is far from new! Trumbull found the streets of St Peter Port 'excessively narrow… very dirty and nasty'. He considered that there was need of a good quay and that there was scope for constructing vaulted cellars. However, he did approve of the fine pier. That apart, he found the town

> has nothing remarkable in or about it, the houses generally not built for ornament but present use, without ceilings and with most untoward chimneys; generally stocked with stocking merchants as they will call themselves, those that buy all the stockings that are made in the Island and barter or sell them away by wholesale in France. The stockings are generally of a finer sort than those in Jersey, some of them so curiously knit and so fine that they may be drawn through a ring, and worth 20 shillings or 30 shillings, which wool they have also liberty to transport from England…

The islanders were proud of any silver that they possessed –

> I observed abundance of silver drinking plate in most houses, which is a general prevailing ambition among them, and some scarce worth a penny or money to buy bread have £8 or £10 worth of plate, which they take pride in showing upon all occasions.

At this time the merchants of St Malo were bringing large quantities of silver from Spain and this was probably the source of much of the island silver-ware.

At the Town church Trumbull found excellent singing of the French psalms

> so harmoniously and with such evenness and judgement and with universality that the music of our choirs seems inferior to theirs.

He noticed 'just above the town' a large field that they called a green and employed it to bowl.

During the 1680s the French king revoked the Edict of Nantes and persecuted Protestants. Many fled to the Channel Islands, some seeing the islands as a stepping-stone to asylum in England but others settled permanently. Some of the families had links with the Huguenot mercantile network in Europe and America. This was valuable to the development of St Peter Port as an international entrepôt.

From 1689 until 1697 and from 1702 until 1713 Britain was at war with France. From 1689 the Channel Islands were no longer considered neutral and the islanders helped the new British monarchs William and Mary by engaging in privateering. Privateering has often been confused with piracy. In fact the two activities were quite separate. Piracy was condemned by the maritime powers and pirates faced summary execution. Privateers were the captains of privately-owned vessels who held a letter-of-marque issued by the Admiralty. The letter-of-marque entitled the privateer to operate against the shipping of a designated enemy. Privateers aimed to capture enemy cargo ships. These 'prizes' were then taken to a home port and an Admiralty court would try the case, to determine whether the prize had been taken legitimately within the terms of international maritime law. If the prize was legitimate, the proceeds were shared by the captain, crew, owner, and the investors in the enterprise.

Initially the Guernsey captains and ship-owners were slow to take to privateering. However, the sea-farers of St Malo were enthusiastic *corsaires* and the Islanders followed. Between 1702 and 1713 the High Court of Admiralty in London issued 185 letters-of-marque to Guernsey captains. Nearly eight hundred prize vessels were captured during that period. The late Professor Bromley calculated that the gain to Guernsey may have been in the order of £100,000 – a considerable sum in those days. The historian Jonathan Duncan recognized the significance of privateering –

> For the first time in its annals, the island was enabled to export commodities of high value. English merchants came over to purchase French goods captured by the privateers, and particularly brandies, which met with a ready sale. When peace was restored, new ideas of trade gradually developed themselves among the inhabitants, who had now acquired some capital (Duncan 1841, p.232).

Families such as the Careys, le Mesuriers, Tuppers, Bonamys, and Dobrées benefitted from this capital accumulation and prospered as merchants throughout the 18th century. As Britain was frequently at war with France and Spain during the Georgian era, the Guernsey merchants enjoyed further opportunities for privateering in the years 1739-1748, 1756-1763, 1777-1783, 1793-1801, 1803-1814.

6. Georgian prosperity

From the seventeenth century through to the nineteenth century England and several other European states practised mercantilist policies. To prevent the home market from being flooded with foreign imports, high tariff barriers were erected. The merchants of St Peter Port were able to profit from this situation. They created an entrepôt and imported large volumes of spirits, wines, tobacco, tea, and other luxury goods into St Peter Port which served as a large 'duty free' harbour in the English Channel.

These cargoes were stored in the town in some thirty to forty large warehouses and were re-sold to visiting traders. The traders then smuggled the goods into France and England. The French particularly sought tobacco. Brisk business at the harbour created work and this attracted migrants with specialist skills. There was work for anchor smiths, blacksmiths, block-spar-pump makers, carpenters, chandlers, ironmongers, rope-makers, sail-makers, and ship-smiths. By the 1790s about six hundred coopers in St Peter Port were making barrels and about one thousand people worked in factories, cleaning and preparing tobacco for sale to the French. The growing population and visiting sailors kept bakers, butchers, and tavern-keepers busy.

There were some sixty merchant houses in St Peter Port which engaged in the entrepôt business. As the merchants and their families became increasingly wealthy, they engaged in conspicuous consumption. They bought fashionable clothes, ate more lavishly, entertained liberally, and sought amusements. Migrants came to St Peter Port to cater to these new habits of luxury. Artists, actors, musicians, cabinet-makers, dressmakers, hairdressers, porcelain-sellers, and tailors arrived. Between 1750 and 1800 the population of St Peter Port doubled to ten thousand.

The Georgian era witnessed significant urban improvements. In 1742 the Town Hospital was built. The name belies the nature of the institution, it was a workhouse with a rigorous régime. The inmates were given tasks (such as rope-making) that were useful to the merchants and their shipping interests. In the 1760s Cambridge Park was levelled to create a drill-ground for the militia and to create walks for the fashionable. With commanding views over the town, sea, and neighbouring islands, the park proved popular with Islanders and visitors.

From medieval times the island market had been held in the High Street area. Here countryfolk set out fruit and vegetables on matting, and meat was butchered at Cow Lane. This made the High Street look unsightly, at least to Islanders conscious of urban fashionability elsewhere. A new market was proposed and eventually built in the early 1780s. This project created the opportunity to construct assembly rooms above the market. The timing was propitious. Fort George was being built just to the south of St Peter Port to house a larger garrison. The new assembly rooms afforded a perfect venue for the introduction of eligible English army officers to the daughters of Guernsey merchants.

English captains frequently touched at St Peter Port to take on board duty-free alcohol prior to their long voyages. Captain Dixon was impressed only by the cleanliness of the streets of St Peter Port –

> …it consists of several streets, which are dark, narrow, and inconvenient, but always clean, not only on account of their hard bottoms, but also their declivity; so that any dirt or filth is always washed away by the last shower of rain.
>
> The houses in general are built of a coarse kind of free-stone, and seldom appear commodious, but never elegant; indeed convenience alone seems to have been principally attended to, even in their most modern ones. (Dixon 1789 p. 14).

Dixon saw the old St Peter Port. Soon after his visit wealthy families were busy with building projects. The Le Marchant family released land to the west of the town, allowing St Peter Port to burst its medieval corset. The newly-freed land soon accommodated a theatre, chapel, and courthouse. Further to the west Peter de Havilland developed 'New Town' – a commercial enterprise modelled on English precedents.

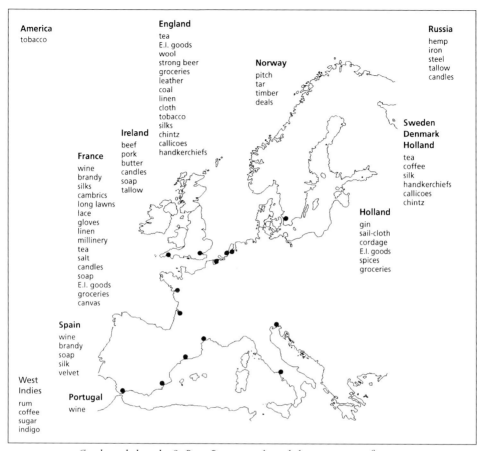

Goods traded in the St Peter Port entrepôt and their countries of origin.

As the town extended westward, it simultaneously re-organized itself internally. Families left the High Street and Pollet, and moved to the suburbs. They abandoned the filth, noise, and crowds of the streets for a more agreeable semi-rural existence.

There was much business in St Peter Port during the wars with France (1793-1815). The garrison was strengthened, and the British navy patrolled local waters. Neutral shipping carried cargoes to and from the port. French spies – real and imagined – were suspected. English actors presented plays at the new theatre built by John Bernard. Edmund Kean spent a season playing here just before journeying to London and national celebrity. Portrait painters found a ready market. Rosetti, a French refugee, organised fashionable soirées at the Assembly Rooms. Elizabeth Ham, a visitor from Dorset, recollected –

> In those days the officers of the Garrison always gave a Ball on the 4th of June, the king's birthday. These balls always caused great heart-burnings from their exclusiveness… Whilst we were dancing some of the ill-natured excluded threw squibs and crackers through the open windows (Gillett 1945, p. 169).

For a while Russian troops – allies of the British – were quartered here. According to local tradition they clambered up the newly installed street lamps and drank the oil. There were also contingents of French Royalist troops who found a temporary home while they planned a counter-revolution. French Catholic refugees abounded and a simple place of worship was arranged at Tower Hill.

7. Regency chic

In the Regency period the Grange became the most prestigious area of the town. Architects were employed to design handsome houses in classical idioms. Doric columns, Ionic volutes, and Egyptian motifs blossomed in a riot of mingled (and mangled) stylistic flourishes. Leading families such as the Brocks, Careys, de Jerseys, Maingays, and Le Marchants were able to guard their privacy, their homes girdled with gardens, hedged and fenced. The proletariat were at a safe distance downtown, near the harbour and market. The French Revolution had inculcated a healthy fear of the *canaille*. The 'New Town' and Doyle Road, peopled by a respectable bourgeoisie, provided the aristocrats with a further buffer.

The States of Guernsey became increasingly involved in urban development. They arranged the building of a prison in 1809 by levying a tax on corn. In 1816 a committee recommended that the States should issue notes of £1 to the value of £6000 and that these notes would be available for the payment of the new market in St Peter Port and various other projects. The scheme involved the redemption of the bank notes by rents, lotteries, and duties. A large capital sum was raised without any interest being paid. The new markets were designed by John Wilson and replaced a warren of medieval buildings. The meat market was opened in 1822, the fish market in 1830.

John Wilson was the architect *par excellence* in late Georgian Guernsey. He oversaw the building of St James' church – created specifically for the Anglican rite to be celebrated in English for the benefit of the Anglophone immigrants – Elizabeth College, and a host of private dwellings – Bonamy House, Castle Carey, Roseneath, and Springfield in particular.

The States were proud of the markets and claimed that the work 'had excited in all classes a similar sense of improvement.' They noted that 401 houses had been built in the town parish between 1819-1829. In 1830 James and George Le Boutillier financed an ambitious scheme near the Markets. They demolished the medieval houses in rue Tanquoel, levelled part of the hill, and constructed the Commercial Arcade. The project involved the carting of 120,000 loads of earth and gravel and 6,000 loads of stone to the South Beach. The scheme bankrupted the Le Boutilliers and the Arcade was not covered as had been intended.

Influxes of migrants in the late Georgian era brought religious change. Several nonconformist chapels were built. The Catholic community left their temporary church at Tower Hill (see above) and built Notre Dame church (1829). In 1851 a second Catholic Church – St. Joseph's Church – was opened. It was designed by Augustus Pugin and is of considerable architectural importance.

8. Victorian progress

As more and more migrants arrived, so English increasingly became the language of St Peter Port. Patois place-names were supplanted. British Royalty inspired memorials and names – Albert Pier, Albert Road, Albert Statue, Cambridge Park, Queen's Road, Victoria Avenue, Victoria Pier, Victoria Road, Victoria Statue, Victoria Terrace, Victoria Tower. St Peter Port displayed the hallmarks of the British Empire, the Islanders showing themselves staunchly loyal to the crown (while vigorously defending their independence from British politicians). Imperial conflicts were commemorated with a gun brought from the Crimea (at the Arsenal) and a Boer War memorial (in St Julian's Avenue).

The Victorian era saw improvements in transport. Steamships made their first appearance in local waters in the 1820s. With the coming of railway services to Southampton and Weymouth in the 1840s it became possible for travellers from London and the Midlands to reach St Peter Port in greater comfort and more quickly. Thanks to well-integrated rail and ship timetables, thousands of English tourists flocked across each year.

There were urban improvements throughout the century. The Guernsey Gas Company was founded in 1823 and brought improved lighting to the town. Anthony Trollope the novelist visited the Channel Islands on behalf of the General Post Office and here invented pillar-boxes. In 1853 boxes were installed in Hauteville, Union Street, the Piette, Colborne Place, the Gravées, and Elm Grove. The boxes were to be cleared every weekday. The box at Union Street still stands and is the oldest box in the British Isles still in use. In 1858 the Channel Islands Electric Telegraph Company laid a cable linking England to the Channel Islands. The Guernsey telegraph office was sited at the Guard House, South Pier, St Peter Port.

In the mid 19th century St Peter Port underwent an excellent transformation. Formerly there had been a nasty little harbour spewing out pestilential exhalations, the narrow quay was just wide enough to allow two carts to pass, and refuse was dumped every day at either end. By the 1860s guide books were celebrating a fine new harbour, a new lighthouse, magnificent jetties, superb gardens, a bathing pool for men, spacious quays with an artistic masterpiece – a colossal statue of Prince Albert.

The horse-drawn omnibus gave way to trams. The Guernsey Steam Tramway Company opened its service in 1879 and linked St Peter Port to St Sampson's. The company was replaced by the Guernsey Railway, virtually an electric tramway, in 1892. In 1887 a dynamo was used to generate street lighting in front of Randall's Brewery in the Avenue. Eleven years later Edmundson's Electricity Corporation was granted the concession to build and operate an electricity supply in Guernsey. By February 1900 150kw could be generated from the power station at Les Amballes, St Peter Port.

St Peter Port experienced little demographic growth during the Victorian era, its population hovered between 15,000 to 18,000. These population figures, however, conceal important flows of migrants. There were Islanders who emigrated to Canada, Australia, New Zealand; they were replaced by incoming Britons, invalids and pensioners, drawn by the mildness of the climate and the comparatively low cost of living. Some French, Irish, and English were attracted by work prospects.

Victor Hugo lived in exile in St Peter Port from 1855 until 1870. In 1865 he wrote a chapter about the town for his Introduction to *Les Travailleurs de la mer*. He penned some vivid pictures. The following is an abridged translation of his description.

> In the large square the market women, sitting on the ground in the open air, brave the winter elements… The fishmongers are better treated than the market gardeners; the fish market, a huge covered area, has marble tables with a magnificent display of Guernsey fish, often of miraculous standard. There is a mechanical and literary society. There is a college. They build as many churches as they can… The catholic Irish swarm, short in patience, so that theological discussions are sometimes punctuated by orthodox punches.
>
> Everything is allowed – apart from drinking a glass of beer on Sunday. Sunday law – singing without drinking.
>
> The Faubourg Saint-Germain in Guernsey is called the Rohais. Fine, well-planned streets are common there, all punctuated with gardens. In St Peter Port there are as many trees as roofs, more nests than houses, more noise from birds than vehicles. The Rohais has the patrician appearance of the aristocratic parts of London, white and clean.
>
> Cross a valley, stride over Mill Street, plunge into a sort of gash between two high houses, climb a narrow, endless flight of steps with tortuous angles and shaky flagstones, and you're in a Bedouin town: hovels, sludge, unpaved alleys, burnt gables, staved-in lodgings, abandoned rooms lacking doors and windows, where grass sprouts up, beams straddle the street, ruins block the way, here and there an inhabited shanty, small naked boys, pale women; you might think yourself in Zaatcha.
>
> Some women go from door to door, hawking cheap wares bought at bazars or markets… The hawkers are very poor and, with great difficulty, scrape a few pence in their long day.
>
> In the month of May yachts start to arrive, the roadstead is full of pleasure craft, most schooner-rigged, some steam-powered. Cricket is popular, boxing in decline. Temperance societies rule, very usefully let us say. They have their processions and parade their banners with an approach almost masonic that softens even tavern-keepers. You hear publicans tell drunkards 'drink a glass, not a bottle of it.' The people are healthy, bonny and good.
>
> The town prison is often empty. When he has prisoners at Christmas the jailer gives them a little family feast.
>
> The vernacular architecture has rooted fantasies; St Peter Port is loyal to queen, bible, and sash windows. In summer men bathe naked, bathing trunks are considered indecent – they draw attention. Mothers excel in clothing their children; there is

nothing so charming as the variety of little *toilettes* coquettishly contrived. Children wander alone in the streets, the trust is touching and sweet. Toddlers lead babies. In fashion matters Guernsey copies Paris but not always. Sometimes vivid reds or stark blues betray the English influence.

The shipbuilding carpentry here is renowned; the careening hard is chockablock with vessels for repair. The craft are hauled ashore to the sound of flute music. The flute-player, say the master carpenters, is more productive than a workman.

L'Hyvreuse is a wooded lawn comparable to the finest plots of the Champs-Elysées in Paris, with sea-views thrown in. (Hugo 1883).

The Victorians believed passionately in education. A Mechanics' Institute and a Working Men's Association offered educational opportunities to the poor. St Peter Port boasted a number of excellently educated men, some of whom happily gave lectures about scientific and other topics. Many private schools and academies flourished in the town throughout the century. The States of Guernsey became involved in secondary education in 1883 with the opening of the Boys' School at Granville House. Soon the premises were too small to accommodate the growing roll of pupils and in 1894 the hundred and twenty students moved to Brock Road. In 1895 the Girls' Secondary School was opened at Granville House with twenty three students. After two moves the girls found a home in Rosaire Avenue in 1928 when numbers were two hundred and fifty.

9. Modern times

St Peter Port enjoyed a long Victorian autumn but slowly embraced modernism. The cinema arrived in 1896 and "talkies" were screened not long after their creation in 1929. Motor cars were in evidence in the early 1900s and an act of 1908 required their registration. Cars were uncommon in the country parishes but parking had become a town problem by the 1930s.

The peace was rudely shattered in 1940. The Germans did not realise that the islands had been demilitarised and on 28 June 1940 they sent a squadron of bombers which attacked the harbour; 34 islanders were killed. For almost five years the Islanders suffered privations. Great was the joy that erupted on 9 May 1945 when Liberation arrived. Slowly the town repaired itself. The States of Guernsey used the fiscal independence of the island to fashion an environment favourable to international finance. The town became host to banks and insurance companies. Many of these businesses situated themselves in the Bordage and Truchot – almost precisely where the merchants' warehouses had flourished in the 18th century.

Today St Peter Port faces some challenges. These have been well adumbrated by Tony Le Gallienne who identifies the problems inherent in the competing interests of the different agencies, institutions, and departments involved in running the town. He ends on a positive note:

But I am being far too negative – we have a high street which keeps reinventing itself; wonderful Castle Cornet which is used for plays and meetings, and is fascinating to walk around; marquees on the Crown Pier and Albert Pier in the spring and summer for boating regattas and events; the harbour carnival; a refurbished OGH Hotel, and an expanded Fregate Hotel; a redeveloped Royal Hotel Site; the New Market; cafes, restaurants and clubs; a UAP document which is able to say, and we are able to believe, that 'St Peter Port is acknowledged to have one of the finest urban environments in the British Isles'; and a character which comes from its challenging topography, its relationship to the sea and its architecture.

But we could do so much better. (Le Gallienne 2007, p.189).

BIBLIOGRAPHY

Virtually every book about Guernsey history has some relevance to the history of St Peter Port. What follows is necessarily a very brief bibliography. The Société Guernesiaise and the Guernsey Society have a long and distinguished record of publications and their websites should be consulted (http://www.societe.org.gg/about/contact.html; http://www. guernsey-society.org.uk/).

For guided tours consult http://www.visitguernsey.com/guided-walks-tours (All websites accessed 28 August 2016).

Place of publication Guernsey unless otherwise stated.

TSG = Transactions of La Société Guernesiaise. It should be noted that the dates given for the TSG are publication dates. Issues are for a year, the publication date is one year later - e.g. the issue for 2012 was published in 2013.

———————

Actes 1851	Actes des Etats de l'Ile de Guernesey, 1605-1845.
Bolton 1968	Bolton, B. 'Esperkeria congrorum' TSG XVIII/3 pp.288-296.
Brett 1975	Brett, C.E.B., Buildings in the town and parish of St Peter Port.
Carey 1921	Carey, E. 'Social Life in Guernsey in the sixteenth century' TSG VIII/4, pp.243-273.
Carey 1932	Carey, E. 'A Trip to Guernsey in 1798 by W.T. Money' TSG XI/2, pp. 243-273.
Carey 1935	Carey, E. 'The growth of St Peter Port in the early 19th century from the MS of the late F. C. Lukis, Esq.' TSG XII/ 2, pp.151-170.
Cox 1908	Cox, C. 'St Peter Port in bygone times' TSG V/3 pp.333-348.
Cox 1999	Cox, G. Stevens St Peter Port 1680-1830. Woodbridge.
Cox 2009	Cox, G. Stevens The Guernsey Merchants and their World in the Georgian era.
Cox 2012	Cox, G. Stevens Guernsey's Medieval Castles.
Cox 2013 a	Cox, G. Stevens The Church in Guernsey 1000 AD – 1500 AD.
Cox 2013 b	Cox, G. Stevens Pugin & Guernsey.
Cox 2014	Cox, G. Stevens Social Life in Georgian Guernsey.
Cox 2016	Cox, G Stevens Victor Hugo's Guernsey Neighbours.
Crossan 2008	Crossan, R-M Guernsey, 1814-1914: Migration and Modernisation. Woodbridge.

Crossan 2015   Crossan, R-M *Poverty and Welfare in Guernsey, 1560-2015.* Woodbridge.

Eaglestone 1949   Eaglestone, A. J. *The Channel Islands under Tudor Government.* Cambridge.

Enquiry 1824   *Enquiry into the present state and condition of Elizabeth College, at Guernsey.*

Favela-Stevens 2011   Favela-Stevens, N. *St. Peter Port in the Golden Age of the Postcard.*

Gillett 1945   Gillett, E. W. *Elizabeth Ham by Herself, 1783-1820* London

Grubiak 1960   Grubiak, O. & J. *The Guernsey Experiment.* Hawthorne, California.

Hocart 1984   Hocart, R. 'A Guernsey merchant in the reign of George II – Nicholas Dobrée' TSG XXI/3, pp. 360-378.

Hocart 1985   Hocart, R.'The Journal of Charles Trumbull' TSG XXI/ 4, pp. 566-585.

Hocart 1993   Hocart, R. 'The Building of the New Town' TSG XXIII/ 2, pp. 342-377.

Hugo 1883   Hugo, V. *L'Archipel de la Manche.* Paris.

Jamieson A.G. 1986   Jamieson A.G. *A People of the Sea.* London.

Kellett-Smith 1981   Kellett-Smith, S.K. 'The Guernsey Cholera epidemic of 1832' TSG XX/5, pp. 643-655.

Le Gallienne 2007   Gallienne, T. *Guernsey in the 21st Century.*

Le Patourel 1935   Le Patourel, J. 'The Early History of St Peter Port' TSG XII/2, pp. 171-209.

Le Patourel 1937   Le Patourel, J. *Medieval Administration of the Channel Islands.* Oxford.

Le Patourel 1955   Le Patourel. J & J. 'Castle Cornet: Excavations, 1953'.TSG XV/5 pp. 350-361.

Le Patourel 1958   Le Patourel, J. *The Building of Castle Cornet.* Guernsey

Lespagnol 1990   Lespagnol, A. *Messieurs de Saint-Malo Une élite négociante au temps de Louis XIV.* Rennes.

Little 1963   Little, B. *St. Peter Port its story and its buildings.*

Marr 1987   Marr, J. *Guernsey Bailiwick Harbours and Landing Places c.2000B.C. to 1987.*

Niven 2016   Niven, P. *St. James, Guernsey.*

Ogier 1996   Ogier, D.M. *Reformation and Society in Guernsey.* Woodbridge.

Ogier 1998   Ogier, D.M. 'Night Revels and Werewolfery in Calvinist Guernsey' Folklore 109.

Ogier 2009   Ogier, D.M. 'Glimpses of the Obscure: the witch trials of the Channel Islands' in A. McShane and G. Walker (ed.), *The Extraordinary in Everyday Life in Seventeenth-Century England: essays in celebration of the work of Bernard Capp.* (London, 2009).

Ordonnances 1852   *Recueil d'Ordonnances de la Cour Royale de l'Isle de Guernesey, 1533-1840.*

Priaulx 1962   Priaulx T.F. 'The Guernsey stocking export trade in the 17th century' XVII/2 pp. 210-223.

Sharp 1968   Sharp E. 'The Evolution of St Peter Port Harbour' TSG XVIII/2 pp.226-255.

Sharp 1970	Sharp, E. 'The shipbuilders of Guernsey' TSG XVIII/5 pp.478-502.
Stevens 1982	Stevens, P. 'Trollope and the Guernsey Postal Service' TSG XXI/1 pp.103-106.
Tupper 1876	Tupper F.B. *The history of Guernsey and its bailiwick*.
Tyson 1993	Tyson, N. 'Candie Cemetery and its Monuments' TSG XXIII/3, pp.599-626.

NOTES

No town can properly be understood without reference to its immediate hinterland. For this readers should consult Richard Hocart's excellent new book *The Country People of Guernsey and their Agriculture, 1640-1840* (Guernsey, 2016). For place names see H. Lenfestey *Guernsey Place Names* (2014). Little 1963, Brett 1975, and Hocart 1993 deal with the architectural history of the town. It was Little who educated the British public about the charm of St Peter Port. Brett provides miniature biographies of hundreds of the town's buildings. Hocart carefully chronicles the creation of the 'new town.' *At Their Majesties' Service* (Gateway Publishing Ltd, Sark, Channel Islands; 2015) by Colonel Richard Graham tells the constitutional history of Guernsey and relates it to the houses occupied by the Governors and Lieutenant-Governors over the centuries. These building were virtually all in St Peter Port.

1. Beginnings – Much important archaeological excavation has been conducted in recent years by Dr Heather Sebire, Dr Jason Monaghan, and Dr Philip de Jersey. The story is best followed by visiting Candie Museum and consulting recent issues of the *Transactions of the Société Guernesiaise*.

2. Medieval – The best discussion of medieval St Peter Port is Le Patourel 1935. The present author is heavily indebted to that excellent essay. *Pace* the title, Carey 1921 is relevant to the medieval era. For Ivy Castle and Castle Cornet and a discussion of chronology see Cox 2012 and Appendix 1 below. Le Patourel 1937 explains the administrative context.

Hospital – see The National Archives C 143/298/20 (Peter de Sancto Petro of Guernsey to new found a hospital at Bouet (Bowez) in the parish of St. Pierre Port, and to endow it with land and corn-rent there. Inquisition in French, 24 Edward III).

The chapel of the blessed Michael – Cox 1908 p.344.

For the stimulus of a castle in town formation see M. Kowaleski *Medieval Towns A Reader* Toronto 2008, p.21.

3. A Godly town – Ogier 1996, 1998, 2009 are fundamental to an understanding of the period. See also Eaglestone 1949. Le Patourel 1958 provides great detail about the Tudor building programme at Castle Cornet. For the Elizabeth College syllabus see *Enquiry* 1824 Appendix. For rules and regulations about urban life see *Actes* 1851 and *Ordonnances* 1852.

4. Stuart times – Ogier 1996, 1998, 2009. Eaglestone 1949 takes the story down to 1642. For the Civil War era see Tupper 1876.

5. Better days – See Hocart 1985 for the Journal of Charles Trumbull. For St Malo and Guernsey merchants see Lespagnol 1990. Privateering is covered in Jamieson 1986, chapters 5, 6, 7 in particular.

6. Georgian prosperity – Brett 1975; Carey 1932; Cox 1999, 2009, 2014; Hocart 1993.

7. Regency chic – Brett 1975; Carey 1935; Cox 2014; Niven 2016. Interesting light is shed on the late Georgian era in Stephen Foster's forthcoming study – *Zoffany's Daughter: Love and Treachery in a small island* (Blue Ormer, to be published October 2017).

8. Victorian decorum – Crossan 2008 provides deep analysis of demographic issues. Grubiak 1960 details the clever financing of the markets. Kellett-Smith 1981 is a fine account of a cholera crisis, enhanced by the fact that the author was a doctor. Cox 2013b examines Pugin's links with Guernsey, particularly the building of St Joseph's church. Tyson 1993 shows how a cemetery can reveal a lot about a community.

9. Modern era – Le Gallienne 2007.

SITES TO VISIT

It is pleasing to wander through St Peter Port. The reason for this is to be found in *The Concise Townscape* by Gordon Cullen (1971) who explains the aesthetic principles that make a town 'work' architecturally. St Peter Port happily exemplifies many of the features lauded by Cullen: – 'serial vision' – a developing view as one progresses through the town; 'lines of force'– the coast and the hills; closure effected by irregularity or asymmetry of layout; a cross as focal point; trees and gardens; changes of level; 'here and there' – an articulated environment resulting from the breaking-up of flow into action and rest, into corridor street and market place, alley and square.

The following is a brief summary of buildings worthy of attention. Brett 1975 amply demonstrates that there are many more.

Medieval – Ivy Castle, Castle Cornet, Town Church.

Tudor – Castle Cornet – the Mewtis Bulwark in particular. Buildings at the bottom of Berthelot Street. The JT building in High Street has been much restored over the centuries but it still gives an impression of the Tudor style of building. The text above the door (dated 16 October 1578) is a reproduction; the original is to be found in the Guille-Allès library. Several buildings overlooking the harbour have cellars dating back to this era.

Stuart – Castle Cornet.

Georgian – Hospital (now the police station) – l'Hyvreuse (Cambridge Park) – Assembly room (now the Guille-Alles Library) – Greenhouse at Candie Gardens – Constables' Office – Moore's Hotel – Royal Court – New Town – St James' church – Elizabeth College – The Grange – Castle Carey – Commercial Arcade.

Victorian – Victoria Tower – Candie Cemetery – St Joseph's – Albert statue – the outer harbour – the markets.

Modern – Notre Dame church, Occupation Memorial.

APPENDIX 1

The medieval castles of Guernsey and their chronology

The account of castle building advanced in section 2 is my own and it should be understood that it challenges that advanced by some archaeologists. I laid out my arguments in Cox 2012. This is a brief recapitulation with some revisions. The monograph should be consulted for a fuller discussion and references.

The reasons for calling Ivy Castle a <u>royal</u> castle are:
— it was situated on land belonging to *fief le roi*;
— there are references to the king appointing a chaplain to it;
— there was a strong folk memory, recorded by royal commissioners in the seventeenth century, of the castle having been used as the seat of the Captains and Governors of this isle.

In 1244 Henry III instructed Drew de Barentin to allow the chaplain to have for life his grazing around the <u>old</u> castle of Guernsey. Richard Hocart argues, correctly in my opinion, that the grazing rights identify the castle as being Ivy Castle, grazing rights at the sea-bound Castle Cornet are difficult to envisage. The adjective 'old' was used – I suggest – to distinguish Ivy Castle, the <u>old</u> castle, from the <u>new</u> castle – Castle Cornet.

Evidence from the Liberate Roll suggests that there was castle-building in Guernsey in the 1240s and the details fit Castle Cornet rather than Ivy Castle. Archaeological evidence suggests that building work was carried out at Castle Cornet in the 1270s. This I interpret as an enlargement and strengthening of the castle.

The fourteenth century saw many troubled years. In the 1320s a castle of refuge was developed at Jerbourg. Then, in 1350, Edward III ordered the construction of a strong wall to defend St Peter Port. Historians and archaeologists have long debated whether a wall was built. Certainly a tower was constructed – La Tour Beauregard – and its garrison was on hand to help the townsfolk in the event of an attack.

Circa 1403 John Newenham petitioned the crown (TNA, SC 8/217/10824, incorrectly cited in Cox 2012. The TNA re-dated the Newenham petition to *circa* 1403). The petition stated that 'certain people of Guernsey have built towers and fortresses without the king's permission, for reasons unknown, and have also withheld the custom of the sea belonging to the king. He therefore requests that the council either order the bailiff and jurats of the island to resist such matters and prevent further ones being done, or that they write separately to the trespassers to appear and answer the charges'. The petition bears the endorsement: 'Let writs be issued under the great seal with the assent of the council to Cleremond, Bernard, Fever and Fever, ordering them to be before the council at the quindene of Michaelmas next, under pain of £100 each.' The named trespassers were Gerveys Cleremond; John Bernard; John Fever the elder; Gylot Fever.

The date is significant. Jonathan Sumption records that in 1403 the Bretons assembled a fleet of armed merchantmen at Morlaix. At the beginning of August they sailed against the English coast and inflicted great damage at Plymouth. Heading homewards, the Bretons landed on Guernsey and Jersey, wreaking destruction and exacting heavy *patis* from the inhabitants (J. Sumption, *Cursed Kings The Hundred Years War* IV, 2015, p. 109). The towers and fortresses mentioned by Newenham refer, I suggest, to the building of castles of refuge – Corbière Castle and Vale Castle – in the aftermath of the Breton raid.

Professor Le Patourel saw Vale Castle as a medieval building. Some archaeologists have dated it later on the basis of artefacts found there. If Vale Castle was built as a castle of refuge *but rarely if ever used as such*, the search for artefacts to date it may be in vain. In Cox 2012 I speculated that Vale Castle dated from unrest later in the fifteenth century. I am now inclined to think that it is one of the castles referred to in TNA, SC 8/217/10824.

Corbière Castle also appears to have been a medieval fortification. By the early 17th century stone was being robbed from it. The current researches of Lord Eric de Saumarez, Dr Philip de Jersey, and Richard Heaume confirm a medieval date.

If Newenham's statement does refer to these castles, we have the happy knowledge of knowing who instigated them – Gerveys Cleremond; John Bernard; John Fever the elder; Gylot Fever. There is a Claremont cottage located not far from the Vale Castle. It is just possible that the name is ultimately derived from Cleremond.

The Author

Gregory Stevens Cox was born in Ilchester and educated at Beaminster Grammar School. He read Classics and Oriental Languages at St John's College, Oxford University, and subsequently became a schoolmaster in Guernsey. He was awarded a Master's degree (with distinction) by Exeter University for research into the teaching of local history in Guernsey; and a doctorate by Leicester University for his study – *St Peter Port 1680-1830*.

In the 1990s he regularly showed visitors around the town and prepared an advisory report about historic St Peter Port and tourism for the States of Guernsey. In 2014 he was awarded the MBE for his services to Guernsey culture and history. He was the co-founder of the *Victor Hugo in Guernsey Society* and helped to mount the festival in 2016 that celebrated the 150th anniversary of the publication of Hugo's novel *les Travailleurs de la mer* (set in Guernsey).

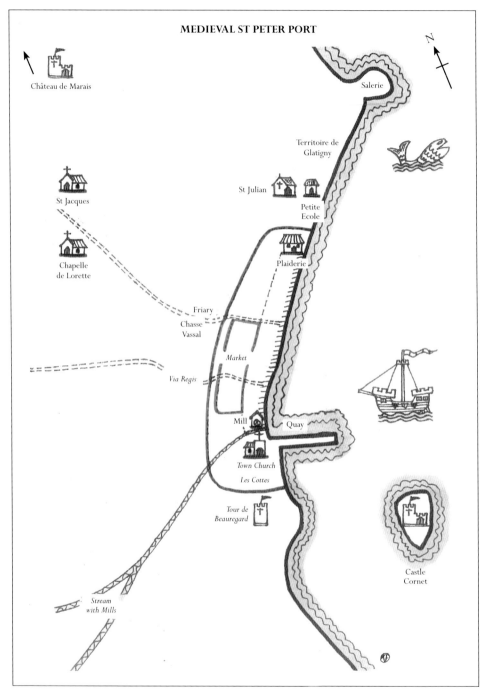

MEDIEVAL ST PETER PORT

Château de Marais

Salerie

Territoire de
Glatigny

St Jacques

St Julian

Petite
Ecole

Chapelle
de Lorette

Plaiderie

Friary

Chasse
Vassal

Market

Via Regis

Mill

Quay

Town Church

Les Cottes

*Tour de
Beauregard*

Castle
Cornet

*Stream
with Mills*

St Peter Port in the 15th century.

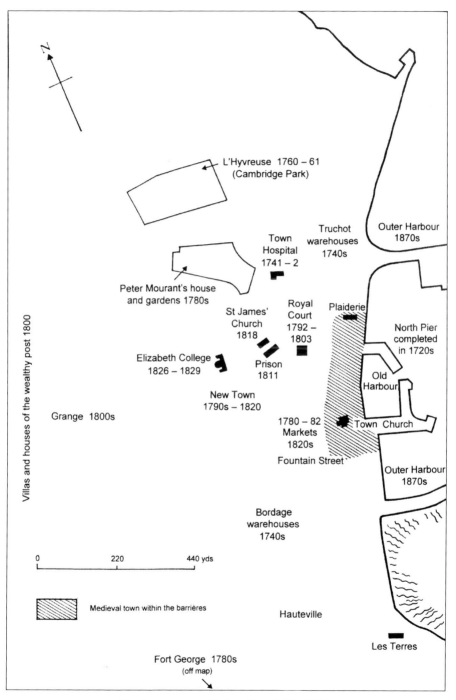

The development of St Peter Port 1680-1830.

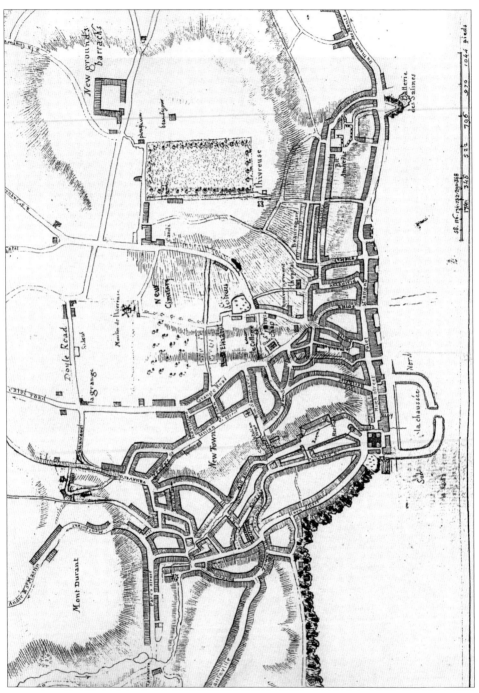

St Peter Port, early 19th century. Priaulx Library, de Magnac ms.

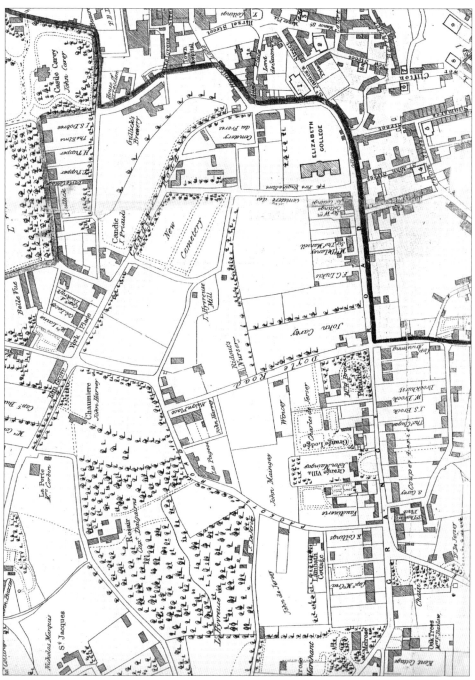

St Peter Port — the Grange. Detail from The Town of St Peter Port and its Environs.
Turner & Co, Edinburgh, 1843.

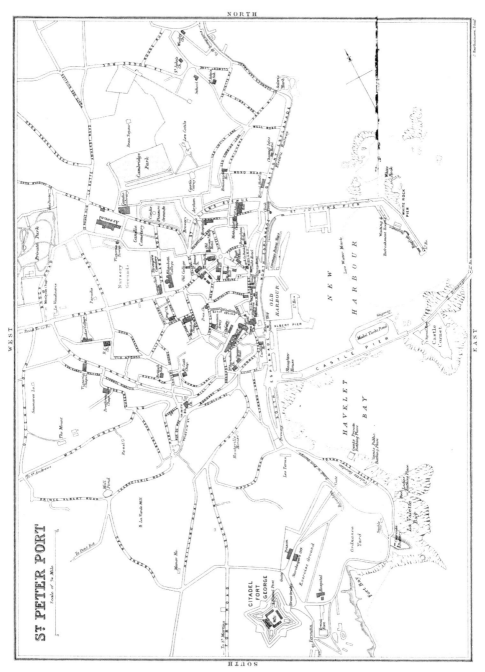

St Peter Port, late Victorian era.

The town church. Much of the building dates from the 14th-15th centuries.

Berthelot Street, a nineteenth century photograph illustrating a typical Tudor house.

The grand town house of the de Saumarez family, built circa 1760.

William Le Marchant's house built in 1787. Now the Constables' Office.

St James' Church. Designed by John Wilson and built in 1818 as a place of worship with services in English for the benefit of the many British immigrants. 'An extremely important and handsome specimen of the neo-classical style' (Brett 1975, p. 42).

Millmount 'A very good three-bay two-storey white-painted stucco house, with Georgian glazing, balcony, awning carried on eight odd capital-less reeded columns, semi-circular trellis above the balcony, canted triple-windows below; a small later addendum in Tudorish style to the east; a very good ironwork garden arch, with lamp-bracket' (Brett 1975, p. 56).

GEORGIAN ELEGANCE

When W.B.H. Rowley's house and contents were sold by auction a detailed inventory was published in l'Indépendance (17 January 1829). This affords a glimpse inside Belle Vue House at the New Ground (Cambridge Park). The reconstruction is by Mikal Dyas — to whom my thanks. ⟶

Grange Lodge – designed by John Wilson, 'a pretty piece of battlemented neo-Tudor nonsense'
(Brett 1975 p. 45)

LONDON TO THE CHANNEL ISLANDS

Via POOLE, in TWELVE HOURS,
WITH A BAG OF LETTERS FROM H. M. POST OFFICE.

Alteration of Time on and after Aug. 1.

Passengers and Baggage via POOLE avoid Dock and Pier Dues.

Goods by this route are free of Dock and Pier Dues.---Freight and Rail Charges same as via Southampton.

THE NEW STEAM COMPANY'S

SOUTH-WESTERN NAVIGATION UNRIVALLED

STEAM SHIPS,

Will Leave POOLE HARBOUR,

WITH GOODS AND PASSENGERS, FOR

GUERNSEY & JERSEY

Every **MONDAY** and **THURSDAY** Nights, at **ELEVEN** o'Clock, Immediately after the arrival of the Up Mail Train from Dorchester:

Returning from **JERSEY**, every **WEDNESDAY** Afternoon, at Three o'clock, and **SATURDAY** Morning, at Eight o'clock.

The Passage to or from POOLE and GUERNSEY will not exceed **FIVE HOURS AND A HALF,** THEREBY OFFERING TO THE PUBLIC,

THE MOST RAPID COMMUNICATION BETWEEN THE CHANNEL ISLANDS AND THE METROPOLIS.

FARES to and from LONDON to GUERNSEY and JERSEY, the same as via SOUTHAMPTON, viz:—

First Class Rail & Main Cabin, 35s. 6d.—Second Class Rail & Main Cabin, 31s. 6d. Second Class Rail and Second Cabin, 24s. 6d.—Third Class Rail and second Cabin, 20s. 8d.

BETWEEN POOLE AND GUERNSEY AND JERSEY,—

Main Cabin, 21s.—Fore Cabin, 14s.—Carriages, £3.—Horses, £3.—Dogs, 5s. STEWARD'S FEES.—Main Cabin, 1s.—Fore Cabin, 6d.

1 Cwt. of Personal Baggage is allowed each Chief Cabin Passenger, all above that weight will be charged 6d. per cubic foot.

PASSENGERS EMBARK AND DISEMBARK AT POOLE FREE OF CHARGE.

Goods by the COMPANY'S VESSELS are carried at very REDUCED RATES. To Merchants and Shippers this route offers peculiar ADVANTAGES OVER EVERY OTHER PORT.

Merchandize of every description may be Imported or Exported at the low local rate of 3d. per ton only, while the facilities are equal to any Port in the United Kingdom.

THE COMPANY'S VESSELS LEAVE

JERSEY FOR ST. MALO,

Every TUESDAY Afternoon, returning every **WEDNESDAY** Morning, at Ten o'clock. Also, from

JERSEY TO GRANVILLE,

Every FRIDAY Afternoon, returning every **SATURDAY** Morning, ACCORDING TO TIDE.

The SOUTH-WESTERN RAILWAY COMPANY'S TRAINS leave POOLE for DORCHESTER, Five times daily—from whence Fast Coaches start for BRIDPORT, YEOVIL, TAUNTON, EXETER, &c., &c.

Also, from POOLE first-rate Conveyances for BLANDFORD, SHAFTESBURY, BATH, BRISTOL, &c., &c.

THE NEW SOUTH-WESTERN STEAM NAVIGATION COMPANY will not be responsible for any damage or loss of Baggage, nor for Delays, Accidents, or Sea Risks of any kind whatsoever.

New South-Western Steam Navigation Company's Office, 162, High Street, Poole, July 27th, 1848.

JOHN BROUGHTON, Agent.

LANKESTER, PRINTER, 92, HIGH STREET, POOLE.

Improved communications 1848

Les Arcades, designed by John Wilson, a Victorian photogravure.

Elizabeth college designed by John Wilson, built 1824-29, 'a formidable stucco construction in a sort of Tudor style' (Brett 1975 p.44)

Hauteville House. This was originally the home of the Tuppers, wealthy Guernsey merchants. Victor Hugo bought it in 1856.

de Putron boatyard at Glategny, one of several boatyards situated in the town. Note the gap smashed in the wall to facilitate the launching of the newly-built brig — the Emerald, according to a note on the reverse. © David Family Collection; reproduced by kind permission.

Victoria Tower, built in the late 1840s. 'One of those magnificent splurges of extravagance to which the Victorians were prone' (Brett 1975, p. 57).

Albert Statue by Joseph Durham. A contemporary print illustrating the inauguration in 1863.

The harbour was significantly improved between 1850 and 1870. The new outer harbour afforded berthing for steamships bringing tourists – and taking away tomatoes and fruit.

THIS TABLET IS ERECTED TO THE MEMORY, AND RECORDS THE NAMES OF THOSE MEMBERS OF THE CIVIL POPULATION WHO LOST THEIR LIVES AS THE RESULT OF AN ENEMY AIR RAID ON JUNE 28th 1940.

ANQUETIL, BASIL T.	GILLMORE, FREDERICK R.	MAUDUIT, MARCEL F.
BATISTE, WALTER J.	HEAUME GERALD A.	NORMAN, CECIL C.
BOUGOURD, CLIFFORD H.	HOBBS. HAROLD F.	RENOUF, JOHN R.
BREHAUT, ALICE.	INGROUILLE, HENRY.	ROBERT, AMY L.
BREHAUT, GEORGE E.	LE CHEMINANT, HAROLD C.	ROBERT, DAISY M.
CAMBRIDGE, HERBERT W.	LE MAITRE, HERBERT W.	SARRE, JOHN E.
COLLENETTE, FRANCIS T.	LE NOURY, PIERRE.	SARRE, WALTER.
DE CARIS, FRANK A.	LE PAGE, FRANK J.	STITCHMAN, CHARLES.
DE JAUSSERAND, LILIAN M.	LE PAGE, FRANK J.	TARDIVEL, JOHN F.
DE JAUSSERAND, SAMUEL.	LE PAGE, ROY.	WALKER JOHN W.
FERBRACHE, OLIVE M.	MAHY, JOHN W.	WAY, JOSEPH E.
	MARQUIS, ALFRED.	

IT ALSO COMMEMORATES ALL GUERNSEY CIVILIANS WHO, IN THIS ISLAND OR ELSEWHERE, DIED IN CONSEQUENCE OF HOSTILITIES DURING THE SECOND WORLD WAR 1939 – 1945.

Harbour memorial.

OCCUPATION MEMORIAL

The Guernsey Liberation Monument is a five-metre-high obelisk, designed by the Guernsey artist Eric Snell and modelled on Neolithic monoliths found in Guernsey. It is composed of 50 pieces of Guernsey granite symbolising the fiftieth anniversary of liberation in 1995. The obelisk was precisely placed to mark the path of the Sun on the 9th May 1995, the fiftieth anniversary of the Liberation. The tip of the shadow of the obelisk falls on a curve of stone seating throughout the day, and provides a link between 1945, 1995, and each Liberation Day in the future.

Inscriptions placed on the seating record the major events of the 9th May 1945: the signing of the surrender of the German forces at 7.15 am, the landing of the British Liberating Force at 8.00 am, and the unfurling of the Union Flag at 10.15 am. The mathematical calculations required were carried out by David Le Conte, a member of the local astronomy society, the Astronomy Section of La Société Guernesiaise, using a computer program which he wrote specifically for the purpose. The program, called SunShadow calculated the position of the Sun every five minutes, from 0640 to 1700 hours British Summer Time, for the 9th May 1995, to an accuracy of 1/100th of a degree, and converted the data to coordinates of the tip of the shadow, to an accuracy of just one millimetre. http://www.astronomy. org.gg/liberation.htm

I find this monument remarkable for its simplicity and complexity. Gregory Stevens Cox.

Printed by Creeds Telephone: **01308 423411** Web: **www.creedsuk.com**